I0436903

VIGLETS -
TIME, INFINITY, ETERNITY

VIGGO P. HANSEN

authorHOUSE®

AuthorHouse™
1663 Liberty Drive
Bloomington, IN 47403
www.authorhouse.com
Phone: 1-800-839-8640

©2012 Viggo P. Hansen. All rights reserved.

No part of this book may be reproduced, stored in a retrieval system, or
transmitted by any means without the written permission of the author.

Published by AuthorHouse 08/03/2012

ISBN: 978-1-4772-1144-1 (sc)
ISBN: 978-1-4772-1145-8 (e)

Any people depicted in stock imagery provided by Thinkstock are models,
and such images are being used for illustrative purposes only.
Certain stock imagery © Thinkstock.

This book is printed on acid-free paper.

Because of the dynamic nature of the Internet, any web addresses or links contained in
this book may have changed since publication and may no longer be valid. The views
expressed in this work are solely those of the author and do not necessarily reflect the
views of the publisher, and the publisher hereby disclaims any responsibility for them.

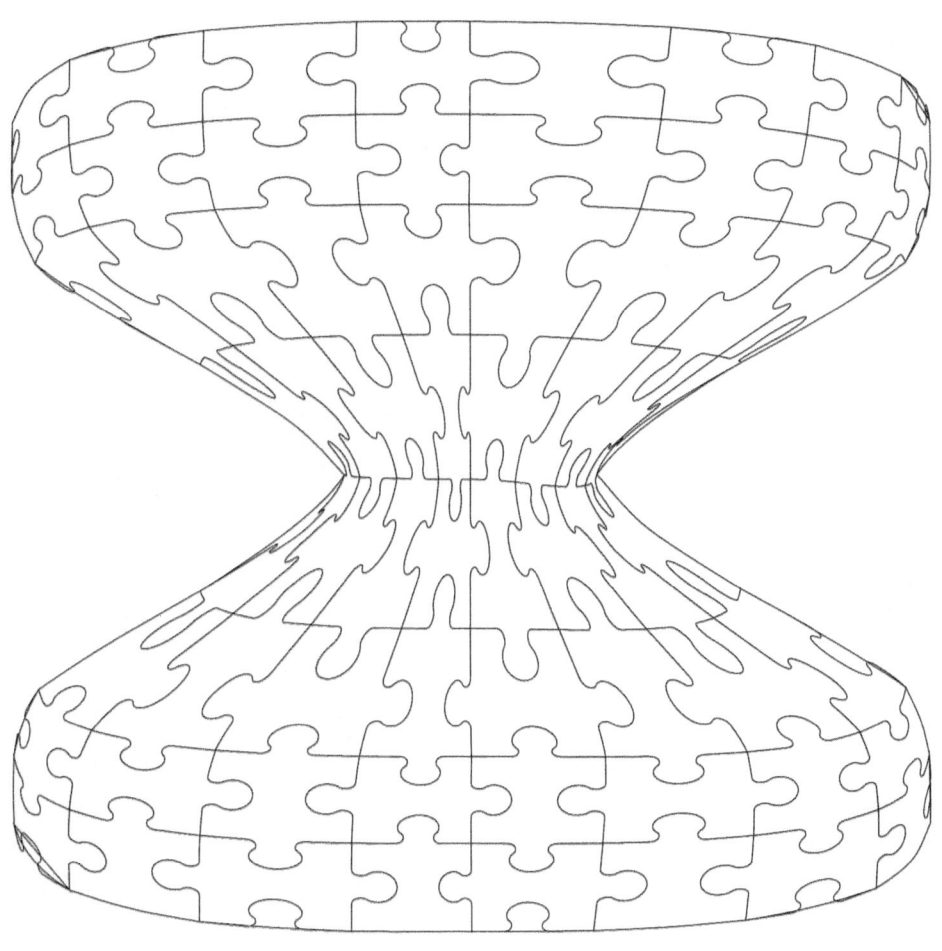

Time in a Bottle?

DEDICATION

To precious family members, dear friends, nice neighbors, former students, colleagues and a random assortment of other living things, maybe even rocks, this third Viglet book is hereby dedicate.

Many life forms, consciously or unconsciously, have contributed to these Viglet reflections on the concepts; time, infinity and eternity.

Special thanks to Dixie Lee, lover, mate, mentor, protector-ess. In addition to family obligations, garden club activities she generously provides inspiration as well as physical and mental guidance. It is her incredible sense of gallows humor (at my expense of course) that makes it all possible.

Being stuck between
A rock and a hard place is easy
Being stuck between time, infinity and one's mate
Is not always so easy.

vph

on any electronic device cornering this market in the near term.

Unfortunately these spooky long range thoughts on what lies ahead have a difficult time taking our minds off - our ever prevailing narcissism, avarice, bodily retention issues, airhead politicians, unscrupulous doctors, and fireball gurus.

> *When the wakeup call comes*
> *We finally realize that*
> *Our true adversary*
> *Was this thing called time*
> *That we had little time for*
> *When we had time.*

Our mortal foe – time – can it be held at bay if human nitwits would focus on its challenges and worry less about amassing "wealth" – be they individuals, nations, corporations or religious orders. Perhaps, if we weren't so preoccupied in killing each other over personal egos gone awry we might develop more profound insights into the preciousness of time.

How frequently have we heard the expression, "I am just killing time?" How smart an idea is that? Killing life's most precious commodity!

What we "idiots" fail to appreciate is that frame, glory and monies are quite paltry when compared to time issues.

To the rescue - Viglets - they help focus and ease the bumpy path to whatever lies ahead - with humor and frivolity. So until we get the bugs ironed out regarding ascension techniques we better start having some down home fun now.

 The humble yet mindboggling mission of Viglets is simply to liberate - seven billion earthly caged human spirits including

After another round more uncomfortable questions flit through our foggy brain – just what is this stuff we call time, infinity and eternity? Do these "concepts" even exist or are they something we all studiously tolerated in order to get a liberal arts degree? Who came up with these notions and more importantly –why?

We do know for damn sure those pesky credit cards do exist and they devilishly define time in no uncertain terms. Wouldn't it be funny if time, infinity and eternity don't exist? What fun – all your balances are paid in full.

This is not meant to in any way deride unpaid Visa, Master, Amex and free Disney "E" ride cards.   These suckers will follow you right to the upper, mid and lower bowels of hell. Thirty days late and you have had it – buster – FICA scores define both hell and eternity.

For most rich Americans, notions about time, infinity and eternity are mere irritations that pop up when; scheduling appointments for kid's braces, setting golf t-times, enjoying Botox injections, trying on new clothes and of course engaging in confused political discussions about education, digging for oil and who to shoot next.

While we can easily relate to these pressing irritants – we simply do not have time - for time, infinity and eternity. But the fact remains - we are inevitably going to have sagging and wrinkled chins, lopsided boobs, way above par golf scores and eventually lose interest in flashier vehicles with more driver apps. These are all distractions – we create – to keep from thinking about time.

Bingo - suddenly a blazingly powerful force arises suggesting we focus on – "Just what is going on down the road apiece?" For sure we will all take this unknown, hopefully happy journey but there are no Google maps currently available. Do not bet

Viggo P. Hansen

Making choices as time moves on
Is everyone's daily challenge
Are they right or wrong – serious or funny?
Someone else will decide
For sure – we all did our best
Bad as they too often were.

The reason I am getting smarter
Is I can't get any dumber
The reason I am getting older
Is I can't get any younger
What a joy – getting smarter and older
Simultaneously
It can't get any better.

When folks lament
They are losing it
Just remember
They probably never had it.

Setting the stage for creating Viglets about Time is easy. As one's RIP era looms like a rapidly rising fuzzy Phoenix out of the ashes of our hilarious past escapades and current dalliances – everyone – begins to ponder three uncomfortable squirrelly topics;

Time - Infinity - Eternity

At first these niggling thoughts are easily doused with a coke, cool beer or scotch on the rocks. But then visions of those who have gone ahead of us "so to speak"" begin to come into clearer focus. Now it is time for a "double" - and "go easy on the water, waiter".

INTRODUCTION

We all need backup plans
Like - if you don't die
Then what?
Or - if you do
Then what?

The underlying theme of the Viglet Movement is best expressed by this pithy Viglet.

Being serious takes you straight to hell
Being funny takes you straight on into heaven.
Being in between is pure misery.
Truly -- it is so.

Viglet III - Time, Infinity and Eternity addresses many things, but the most important messages are:

You can stop getting old-er - now
By creating personal Viglets - now
Nothing to buy - simply spill your guts
In a few personal words - let it all hang out
Then your "Time" will become Infinite.

their caffeine enhanced nervous cells - while simultaneously probing cosmological issues like; what in is going on?

> *With only a three pound glob of gray matter*
> *We can never know much*
> *About our incredible universe*
> *But we can be humble and*
> *Express our feelings of gratitude*
> *With Viglets.*

Viglets – blessed with few grammatical constraints allow their creators freedom to express succinctly and humorously, personal gut level ideas feelings. Though the challenge is uplifting, it is also fun, fun, fun. We are all on this happy go lucky life bus going over the cliff called time. So enjoy - book now.

Your personal Viglet readership audience is boundless and the rewards of creating them translate into a longer and happier existence as you anticipate the infinite.

> *Creating Viglets is*
> *The art of personal story telling*
> *Sharing who you really are*
> *In a few personal words*
> *That will truly last forever.*

> *How can we define time?*
> *By memories & hopes for the future.*
> *Can it be quantified?*
> *Of course not*
> *It can only be enjoyed.*

TABLE OF CONTENTS

Time

What is time, dare you softly whisper,
Reflecting your nervous curiosity?
Is it fine sand flowing in an hour glass, or
Laughing hilariously, or
Weeping over a precious loss, or
Maybe none - or - all of the above.

OK! An opening query.

How often do you really take a brief moment to think about what your time "means" to you - as well as to other living things? For example; what is time for plants living; under water, in water and in the air or ground.

Perhaps time is a beautifully woven fabric
Where each living entity
Be it plant, animal or quiet rock
Is a colorful thread
Carefully woven into an infinite tapestry
Of dreams, hope and happiness
For all - forever.

It would seem that all animals – ranging in sizes from single cell amebas to whales and elephants, in the water, in the ground and in the air have a perspective on time. We can infer that from their routines and behaviors. So – what is the meaning of time for each? This question really hits home with folks afflicted with narcissism. After all for them time is simply them.

Perhaps time is like a freeway or garden path
One can speed or trod along
While enjoying many on and off ramps
Each with new and unique experiences
The journey on the road of time never ends.

Remember yesteryear when
Time was related to
Getting out of the swamp
So we could walk upright
With sciatica, bunions and in stiletto heels.
Ah yes, the good ole days of yore.

Time in tomorrow's world
Will be different
Evolution will make that certain
But can we perhaps today
Play a role in is inevitable coming?
Just Maybe
If you believe in global warming.

Time has infinite standards
That are applicable as needed
To an infinite set of circumstances
And - are meaningful only to each living thing.
Truly mind boggling.

What if earthly animal and plant classifications, along with strange neighbors yet undefined in our universe, all possess this stuff we glibly call life, does this mean each one has a unique sense of what time is? How personal is time?

Just suppose
Each conceivable life form
Concocted a watch to tell time
What would the dial
Look like?

Finally we need to at least recognize rocks. Do rocks have a sense of time? No pun intended but it is hard to tell.

It may be silly
But do rocks have clocks
That go tick tock?
If so – then we need
A Rockex.

If you are truly inquisitive or better yet posses a warped mind (which most of us have), start worrying about the individual components that make up these wonderful, yet inconceivable myriads of "time-life" forms that surround and continually enrich us as they did yesterday and hopefully will in the future. So unless you are a geologist, don't waste your time on rock clocks, unless they are smothered in diamonds.

If these magnificent time keepers are too expensive try the back streets of Bangkok, LA or Chicago. Here time truly does not exist.

There are many fascinating perspectives as to what time is or is not. Since many equations and formulae in the sciences depend upon time – usually written as a small "t", these folks must be assuming there is such a thing as time. For example; $d = rt$, this means that the distance something travels (d) depends on the rate (r) and time (t). This is heady stuff for physicists and first year algebra students. The problems go something like the following.

> *Normal California traffic flow*
> *Eighty miles an hour (r)*
> *Do it for two hours (t)*
> *And you have gone 160 miles (d)*

All well and good, but if there is no "time" then you have gone nowhere – which is just the same as if you are stuck dead on the I-5 headed into Los Angeles – which is usually the case. Since now your rate is zero - you haven't gone anywhere, even if your watch keeps ticking away. Your dreaming about going eighty miles per hour is just that – a dream. This means that if you have neither rate nor time you haven't gone anywhere. On the farm we called this being stuck.

Einstein and his band of clever thinkers even had the audacity to suggest something about that - they postulated that there is no way you farm girls and boys can go faster than the speed of light. Great setting for a Viglet.

> *If Al is right that*
> *The ultimate speed limit is light*
> *Then for sure we need*
> *Some new DMV rules.*
> *But if Al is wrong then we*
> *Don't even need the DMV.*
> *Great – less government.*

Keep in mind that Viglets by design; forgo logic, truth and

transcend confusing and arbitrary rules of grammar, including; weird punctuation, odd ball spelling, and those pesky split dingy dangling things.

Your turn to be frivolous, giddy and even kooky – about time.

My First "Time" Viglet

_____

_____

_____

_____

_____

My Second "Time" Viglet

_____

_____

_____

_____

_____

Time Vignettes

Creating Viglets about the concept of time will quickly and refreshingly take your mind off today's comical political debates, disgusting rich people's economics and theological skirmishes about who's got the worst devil. Parenthetically it is also what keeps micro breweries forever in a bull market - so don't be overly harsh on empty headed politicians, greedy bankers and hallelujah preachers.

> *Historically it was acceptable*
> *To get rich and improve one's life style*
> *Start a political party or religion*
> *You being president or god*
> *Sorry - no longer the case*
> *You now start a brewery*
> *And become - The Brew Master.*

Moving on – there are lots of living things that seem to have a sense of time. Thus we must surely ask - do they have a similar sense of what we humans call time? My guess is that they do - maybe even more profound than ours.

Take the crow – or raven if you are uppity
It knows how to crack nuts and lots of other things
What will happen when it gets a QWERTY keyboard?
I say look out – because it is also stealthy.

How about the snail
The windswept Bristlecone
Or the single cylindered amoeba
All whole new markets for
Rolex, eh?

Rocks are trickier; even though they are made up of the same stuff that keeps the rest of us going, like silicon, carbon and oxygen, which are made up of atoms and other creepy things. It is a challenge, unless you are a gung-ho geologist, to talk about rocks contemplating their next birthday or how old is their grand rock.

Is there a band of frequencies?
Un-dialed and un-tuned
Screaming for our attention
Telling us of an incredible universe
We stubbornly continue to ignore?

Let us for a brief moment entertain the notion that - just maybe - there is a relationship between what life is and what time is, and that we all have different points of view?

For fun, after a libation or two, admit that we are all kin folk - gawd forbid - that is like having dinner with a pig instead of eating him. Since we are all made of the same stuff, are we simply looking at the same rainbow and somehow seeing different colors - like maybe it is all challenged eyesight in the perceiver.

Could time be a rainbow with every life attuned to and seeing different frequencies?

There has always been a bunch of human "Time" thinkers; conjecturing and tinkering about the nature of time. There is evidence that many Chinese, Egyptians, Incas, Greeks, Laplanders, Romans, Swedes and even Danes did nothing else. This was pretty much it for them. They wrote all kinds of things about time, infinity and eternity. An interesting aside, as beer brewing recipes and wine making improved their time thoughts became loftier and loftier.

These guys (it does seem like most of them were kinda lazy males) had cleverly figured out that sitting around contemplating time, was much easier than seeking gainful employment due to lack of useful salable skills. Perhaps they were simply wimps lacking gumption to get into a jam packed arena and poke at each with sharp sticks while riding hapless ponies and large crowds cheered and jeered. Today's analogy is the NFL.

Whatever the reasons these erstwhile "time" mulling philosophers, outhouse attorneys, bankers and theologians, rather than getting day jobs with full benefits, would pine away about time that working stiffs didn't have time for.

Just suppose for a fleeting moment that –

> *Time is a mere mental figment*
> *Begat by lazy brains of yore*
> *To keep from getting their hands dirty*
> *While the real world is indeed timeless*
> *So have we been duped?*
> *Could be- how tragic.*

Today we all wallow in stuff
Most now glibly call time
Nobody knows what in hell it is
But for sure we have all become its
Captives.

While every life seems to have its own sense of time
Humans have all gotten into the same ditch
Where, what we do and when we do it
Is no longer an option
Rather it is a stern regimen
Unknown and undefined.

What finally happened was that these "time thinker" guys became so hassled about their esoteric thoughts without deeds, they decided to do something. They decided to walk their talk – usually a bad idea.

Under these circumstances humans tend to begin to quantifying whatever bothers them. Sure enough they observed there were days and nights – just as all plants and animals recognize. They sensed there was more or less light at different times of the year. Sometimes you had to wear things to stay warm and sometimes you had to go au natural to be cool. The daily starry night shows also seemed to have some regularity.

At the local level, i.e. down on the farm or in the river, something was going on and it seemed to reoccur at intervals that could be predicted. Now the "time thinkers" had both a job and a mission.

Ah ha, there must be patterns. Humans tend to gravitate to things that repeat – that is why we constantly make so many of the same mistakes.

Sticks were stuck in the ground to watch shadows move, ever so slowly. Rocks were piled, bones were carved, and folks, would you believe it sometimes young maidens would dance around poles, naturally with lots of partying. Thrill a minute.

These early horologists were no longer chastised by their fellow farmers, fishermen and berry pickers for being lazy louts. No sir – they had special powers not to be messed with.

Measuring time became respected and today you can pay whatever you want for a bejeweled time piece - a rather sophisticated sundial except it also works at night.

"Time" often seems to reflect people's personalities. You know them all; those that are clock watchers – always on time because they are strapped to glowing atomic clocks complete with nanosecond hands that whiz so fast you can't see them.

Then of course there are the frustrating and intolerable procrastinators – born late, never on time, missing flights and dates and don't know what a clock is unless it is pretty and costs a lot.

And so it is, for some time is a stern task master, while for others it is simply an annoyance and inconvenience imposed on them by others.

Clock watchers see
Time whizzing by rapidly
Procrastinators see only clocks
Whose batteries have died
How lucky they are.

Pessimists see only
The end of time
Optimists see only
On ramps to bigger freeways
With no speed limits.

And so it is with time
At times it drags
Other times it is
Gone in a flash.

If there is such a thing as time
Then our task is to beat the sucker to death
Before it get us
Go team go.

It is said "Never stop the hop"
Eat, drink, love, and be merry
Because tomorrow we will do it again
Hopefully better.

There clearly are many puzzling and challenging aspects to the concept of time – at least as humans have defined it.   Let us consider - how do trees, petunias, monkeys, newts, galaxies, squirrels and geodes view this thing we humans call time? Are we all traveling on this same route that we have called "time" or are they other options?

When watching a sea gull
Gracefully glide over waves and windy shores
You have to wonder
Do they have the same sense of urgency?
Freeway flyers have in getting to the airport?

Statisticians
Love to find averages like
Medians, means and modes
Are there norms for time?

The human concept of time is obviously related to our so called "human brain" - frail as it for sure is. Then we can assume that our mental perceptions define the human's notion of time. Thus – time for other living things may be quite different – it may not even exist. We must be in awe.

Unfortunately and - surely sadly
Humans have assumed
Some kind of silly authority
That they know everything about time
Ask a rock.

The ever napping pussy cats found in barn lofts, a desert trailer park or posh New York condo, as well as the gorgeous dozing lion on the Serengeti, may have a much "better" sense of time than humans. We can only hope.

But since we are the ones with an opposing thumb – and not much else – we should at least be humble in trying to set standards for time and its use. Darn those smart pussy cats.

Kiddy cats and frisky puppies
Along with orchids and river bank violets
Are like stealthy ships in the night
Quietly slithering by each other
In the vast expanse of time
How sad – we may have a lot in common
If we only knew.

Do you ever ponder?
What time meant to the generous hen
Who spent yesterday laying
Your today's omelet?
Probably not – until now.

What really gets one's britches in a knot
Is being gridlocked in traffic
And a cute little snail creeps by
Giving you a grin and a wink
It knows the meaning of time
And you are stuck in it

Then there is all that plant life that sustains all that animal life, with food and oxygen, not to mention social institutions like garden clubs, in spite of Agent Orange abuse. This plant life form incredibly withstands and survives almost anything humans can throw at it – that does raise the question of who is dumber, Amazonia or Wall Street smart asses? How in hell do rutabagas define what humans call time? Their ability to adopt and adapt to an endless set of rocky circumstances in Askov – from hot to cold, hoeing and radiation is for sure marvelous.

The hearty dainty ever yellow dandelions
And awesome regal sequoia trees
Along with the ocean's restless kelp beds
Often seem less stressed
Than gossiping humans in Ritzy hair salons

What is time?
To the ever blooming geranium?
They must be life's ultimate optimists
Since their view of time is simple to
Always bloom and smile.

Or -

Silent seeds in the desert
That may lie dormant
For eons before a shower arrives
Time must truly be a bore
Until a drop of water falls then
Party time.

And -

What is time to the hapless acorn?
Who fell flat on its head one dark night
Woke up wondering if it would
Be eaten by a squirrel
Or become a majestic sequoia tree
Now that is stressful.

Nature gets short shifted
By folks who lack a vision and compassion
Their bold motto is simple – be stupid
Drill baby drill.

We can quickly drift off into esoteric definitions of time for us and every other life form in the universe, but we must remain focused.   It is now your opportunity to:

1. First take a quiet moment to reflect on what time means to you -
2. Then express your ideas about what time is – or isn't
3. By creating your personal Time Viglet.

Keep in mind Viglets forgo and transcend confusing rules of grammar, weird punctuation, odd ball spelling, and those pesky split dingy dangling things.

My Quiet Time Viglet One

_____

_____

_____

_____

_____

My Quiet Time Viglet Two

_____

_____

_____

_____

_____

Infinity

Infinity is letting your soul and mind
Flit joyously and freely among
Old friends, past adventures
Sharing collective hopes for a future
Of countless days yet to come.

Remember the good old number line, where negative infinity is in one direction – endlessly and usually to the left or down - and then the numbers zip through zero heading in the opposite direction called positive infinity, usually to the right or up.

Expressing personal thoughts
About really significant issues
With your simple Viglets
May at first seem daunting
But not so – your thoughts will live forever.
Good or bad – teehee.

Now get ready for a really big ride - far beyond the distant boundaries of our paltry Milky Way galaxy, black holes, Higgs Boson TOEs and bad sauerkraut. We tackle the infinite.

Eventually humans – and perhaps all other life forms -must address the dizzying topic of infinity.   Ah yes, infinity has a timeless twang that many would rather not think about – that is until it is too late or too early. Remember infinity goes both (all) directions. But -

If one's mind is allowed
To wander beyond two dimensions
To an infinite number of dimensions
Be prepared for the ride of your life
No beginning and no end
No matter where you wander.

It is time to ponder –

Suppose time is indeed non existent
And infinity is simply directions
Are we thus going nowhere - really fast?
Not knowing where we are headed
Then even if we never get there
We know not where we came from.
Silly!

The quest here is to mentally pursue new horizons and dimensions, even with limited mental competence. So first – we need some drinks for everyone in the house. Please run a tab, we have a long journey ahead.

Time to ponder
Is it possible?
That without time there are no memories, or
Are there memories only because there is time?
Could it be that time and memories are the same?

It is truly sad that life without good memories is difficult to comprehend and desire. Take a second or two and try to imagine your existence without a single happy memory. It can't be done - so relax.

On the other hand bad memories can created some bad times. Perhaps memory and stuff we call time are part of the same "thing", i.e. the dimension of life and infinity.

For some the notions of time and infinity get mixed up with; relativity, dark matter, worm holes, cosmologies, upset stomachs and hunkered down tweedy coated gurus. The problem arises when they cannot adequately convey their lofty thoughts to the rest of us. We are awed.

Many is the day
When mentally I am far, far away
But then I come back home or office cubical
And what a relief
I still have my old gd problems
They never went away
Now that is true security in understanding time.

Suppose you don't have any problems
Like rich folks with Swiss bank accounts
Who had a lucky run with life's probabilities
For them the perception of infinity
Is yacht hopping forever
For the rest of us it is another day
In the cubicle or on the freeway
We have a different perception of the infinite.

> *And then there those*
> *In pain and loneliness*
> *Whose perception of infinity*
> *We can never understand*
> *Until we become one of them*
> *And then it is too late.*

We are indeed each dealt a variety of cards to play, even though we didn't ante into the game – and could only affort a few chips. Thus the best we can do is express our thoughts with messages that resonate with the infinite – namely our wishes for a better future –

> *Just remember*
> *If things can't get worse*
> *They can only get better.*
> *We are all in it for the "long haul".*

It is said that here is always light at both ends of the tunnel. Whether you look forward or turn around you always see the light.   Never in the dark.

> *Aside from ascension*
> *Which to this day remains poorly engineered*
> *And seldom practiced, like once*
> *The only way to get to the next dimension(s)*
> *Is pretty much by leaving this one*
> *But we can put it off as long as possible*
> *Simply by being nice.*

Your personal Viglets can sometimes be a good reminder when speeding, talking, texting and scratching strange places - while in motion if you simply ask?   "Where in Hades am I going?"

When first getting serious about infinity it seems rather challenging - because in general we are wrestling with esoteric issues that biologically make our skin crawl - even with a shot of Botox.   Just remember that like our precious children - we all get grumpy and edgy on topics that may best be handled while sound asleep. Here you do not have that option.

The nihilists
Who don't believe in time or infinity
Are absolutely the most pathetic
They have nothing going for them
Except one political debate after another
But it is at least good comedy.

It is indeed true
Everyone is on an island of time
Surrounded by a sea of humanity
All sharing a common infinite shore
So why are we polluting and destroying it?

Be glad for the aging process
Hope it lasts infinitely
If it doesn't
You'll be gone
For a long time.

Time to write some Time Viglets on this tricky topic. Nobody knows it better that you and we need to hear it from you.

My Infinity Viglet One

My Infinity Viglet Two

Time – Infinity - Eternity

Circles are endless
Moebious strips are endless
Let us hope all life may be endless
This we often call ETERNITY.

Once humans had conjured up a notion that evolved into something called "Time", it was an easy stretch to suggest it might last forever or - for an eternity.   In the vernacular this idea is sometimes called - to hell and gone.

Infinity and eternity are quite similar as we shall see; theoretically neither has a beginning nor an end, both are embellished in literature with lots of flowery rhetoric. It took awhile for early Neanderthals to recognized this sort of thing, and to this day it remains a bit puzzling to most.

While infinity has a really "cool" symbol - ~ - like a figure eight taking a nap – how appropriate.

If infinity is sound asleep
That presents a challenge
How to be quite
And not wake it up.

Eternity is often given a flora or garden club kind of motif. This is certain most appropriate since the Garden of Eden is by many viewed as the startup point for eternity. It also recognizes the role plants and all animals play in this enterprise called life.

While eternity
Is viewed as forever
Getting on board
May be challenging.

With the notion of infinity you do not need some clever first inning pitch or kick-off event. This has a lot of appeal to those who haven't a clue or give hoot from where they came, which is of course most of us. Furthermore we also have no real clues as to what lies ahead.

Some suggest that
Everything has to have a beginning
Otherwise we wouldn't know where to start
And worse yet
We could never, ever quit
Pumping up IRA accounts.

Most folks with religious proclivities have created elaborate start-up activities – like a; chicken egg, beautiful garden, bolt of lightning, an IPO, metro train station or airport departure terminal. You buy in - get on the bus - take a seat and joyously move in one direction - endlessly. This is relatively easy to do; the simplicity has lots of appeal.

However, let your mind, with or without stimulants and distractions romp around and simply imagine what if - along the journey you step out after leaving the start up station? This is the tricky thing Adam and Eve ran into early on.

This is where human minds become imaginative and create great literature, politics and philosophies, along with pulp magazines and naughty movies; often quite similar.

The next step for our homo sapiens species was to try and convince each other that they, and only they, had the "truth" and nothing but the truth. Facts are damned, skepticism is for wimps – only insiders know what is right for everybody. The central concern is always getting promotion money for some immediate cause – or else.

To insure that the eternity concept never loses its luster, proponents, parents, politicians, dental hygienists, farmers and soothsayers created clever and exciting "marketing" campaigns. In times past this was referred to as lying – but not today – now it is advanced marketing. Mottos tend to be. "Live better by lying".

There are basically two approaches commonly used to get folks thinking about eternity; one is to be scared witless and the other is an award system for being a good guy or gal.

The fear approach is to get folks thinking seriously about eternity by using threats about what happens next if you fail to follow instructions. These techniques - when used on kids goes like this - scare the living bejeesus out of the little nippers until they are about age eight and then they will either never stray or become serial murderers. Ultimate expense to parents or society is about the same – go to college or go to jail, equally cost effective. Some might infer this method has serious implications for education - keep every kid unenlightened and scared. Make a guess where you think dysfunctional politicians come from?

> *Better behave, or*
> *You lose your; I-phone, i-pad or i-balls*
> *Get no French fries with dinner*
> *And may go straight to hell forever*
> *Even before dessert.*

This was more than likely the beginning of teaching the concept of eternity to kids, clean you living space (cave) or rot in hell. If that isn't scary enough how about this - you get to stoke (shovel) furnaces with black dusty lignite coal till "hell freezes over", which is assumed to be a long time. This method is often presented in subtle ways, but clearly demonstrated later in life by advertisements - written mostly by kids who didn't eat their sprouts early on.

The author's guess is that the kids probably wondered what the difference is. However as all parents know these medieval techniques seldom work, on teenagers and above.

The second approach is called positive reinforcement - meaning if you do something considered good you get an award of some kind, like getting to go to the movies with friends, shopping on streets paved with gold, taking a long nap, all night stands with nubile chicks and of course lot-sa money. These awards can't get much better unless you are into bowling.

> *If you are good*
> *And not bad*
> *You can have a sugar less sucker*
> *Or twitter all night long*
> *How nice is that?*

This dichotomy of good and evil helped define time, infinity and eternity. There was good - and then there was evil - hot and cold, yin and his buddy yang, in or out (as in poker and burgers), all reminiscent of the good old zero/one binary system.

Between these polarities you have many winding roads to travel. On the high road you need to decide what being a "good person" really is. You would think this was/is easy, but not so. As a matter of observation – it seems to be getting more difficult by the day.

There has always been an interest in which method is really the most effective. Does scaring kids make them better or does spoiling them make them more virtuous? Both approaches are constantly used in conjunction with eternity.

> *Must we scare, or*
> *Should we spoil*
> *To stay the hell out of hell*
> *And get to that blissful heaven*
> *For stay for eternity.*

On the flip side, it is without doubt much easier to become one of the damned. You simply screw up by being born in the wrong culture, time or place. Today even losing your middle school locker key can make you one of the condemned.

With these happy and not so happy thoughts on eternity, most adults decided to hit on the kids first. Better them than us. Now we have the setting for modern day pedagogy – are our schools chambers of torture or dens decadence?

So where are we? We may have something called time that is often tied with eternity. Then there is infinity which is less personal and works well in mathematics and the sciences.

In summary - our concepts of time, infinity and eternity are often based on explanations made to us as kids by poorly prepared adults and social institutions. Unfortunately childhood is that incredible period in life when really good questions are asked and then generally given rather slipshod answers.

Later on in adulthood, with expanded experiences and knowledge, re-asking these questions becomes more difficult.

The golden age of intellectual life
Is of course early childhood
Questions then are asked unabashedly
But the answers given too often trivial
Worse yet - demeaned.

Time to write your Time Viglets on this tricky topic. Reflect on your own early thoughts about infinity and eternity. How did they begin and how have the evolved. Nobody knows it better that you and we need to hear it from you.

My First Viglet on Eternity

My Second Viglet on Eternity

_____

_____

_____

_____

_____

Historical Vignettes

The sun comes up
The sun goes down
Keep watching this routine
And you'll soon begin piling rocks.

There are many versions on the metrics of recording time, providing it exists, of course. History tells us that good old rock pilers (i.e. people who pile rocks - reminiscent of neo Askovians) had fun watching the sun's rays slink through slits formed by these handmade rock piles.

Those of you who think baseball is a dull sport try sitting around year after year, often in nasty weather, just to watch a light beam flash through a rocky slot. Good news is there was neither scratching of private parts nor spitting all over the pitcher's mound. It was considered a genteel sport.

The reason for referencing this celestial light show business is that it contributed mightily to developing today's concept of time. It worked something like this; devotees, many unemployed, would find and pile rocks, then sit around and drinking tepid home brewed beer for a full year before they would enjoy a momentarily awe inspiring light show, unless it was cloudy – then you simply waited another year. We can only surmise that a year (or more) of solid drinking did make a tiny flashing ray of yellow light between a couple of big pebbles seem like an epiphany.

Even in earlier days before the species realized that you could count forever simply by beginning with one and just keep on trucking, there were observations that when things died they seem to stay dead. Some were confused and concluded this was unacceptable. Living things shouldn't stop – they must just begin doing something elsewhere and keep going.

> *Nothing stops*
> *Everything just keeps going*
> *Where we are not sure*
> *But for sure we keep going*
> *There being no end in sight*
> *We hope.*

Many families, tribes, nations and cultures, as represented and highlighted by their gods, kept their pilgrims "in line" to insure everyone's survival, especially their own. To make these practices palatable, in addition to unsavory fear tactics, elaborate rituals were created.

Flamboyancy was always in vogue, colorful costumes were bedecked with endangered bird feathers and pointy dunce caps made for awe inspiring presentations. Today we find colleges, universities and religions thrive on this pageantry; it is probably a primary reason why so many students even go to college – forget the studies - just savor the pomp and circumstances with flat hats and robes.

Eventually a time came when these earthy cave dwellers began getting a touch of early bohemian style living. This probably coincided with the discovery of beer and wine.

If you are going to indulge
You must do it with class
Don some chicken feathers
Raise your libation while
Looking your partner in the eye
And then boisterously yell "skoal"
To a long and prospers life.

As life kept getting better it was natural that chic females became concerned about their personal appearance, cave décor including, feng shui, fancy curtains, incense burners, line drawings and a trash can.

Our humble cave needs a redo
More color, stick art and moss covered rocks
Expressing today's new designs
Along with a more efficient kitchen
For preparing the days tasty kills.

Unaware of her decorative interests, her smelly hairy mate's concern was focused on why is that uppity homemaker eyeing me while sitting under a bat's nest sporting a shinny greasy coiffure? Obviously her mind is on something that should worry me – "cave remodeling" or as cave guys called it, "cave rehab".

My honey is the cutest
With that nifty dodo bird hairdo
And that far away new furniture look
I am nailed, what can I do to obfuscate?
And inject my male fantasies
Of going fishing.

Timeless furniture
Should not and is not comfortable
Just make it look that way
To keep the neighbors impressed
While not sitting on it
And it will last for eternity.

This was a period in history when infinity was seen as - later tonight baby and then maybe tomorrow we'll catch a fish or two in time for dinner. Time, then as now, has always been related to immediate things like hunger, sex and happy hour.

History rolled on and different kinds of time related issues appeared. "Will this traffic never end, won't my boss shut the hell up, what's with my daughter's forehead tattoo, why are we out of cold beer, the notorious IRS deadlines, when are your folks coming for dinner, etc.?"

History is replete
With time stressors
Waiting patiently is never an option
But being under the gun
Is always the case.

And so throughout history humans looked for ways to escape pressures of time; sleeping is always good, going out and shoot some kin folks will end boredom, indulging in all kinds of funny behavior will do the job, watch rerun TV, play computer games - these activities will surely take you totally out of the world of time. Tweeter folks no longer exist in a world with time. They are long gone.

It is off to Valhalla I go
Ho, ho - ho, ho
With faithful dog Spot by my side
Along with a keg of lager
Computers and its ilk
Are all in the dumpster
I will now be happy for an eternity
Fishing with my dog Spot.

So as we today peer through our smoggy sky of twinkling stars late at night it still seems like they are not that far distant. Their flickering glow certainly gives us a sense of peace, tranquilly, order and hope for an infinite eternity, now that is a double whammy.

The fact that these erstwhile soothing far away lights assuaged rock pilers of yore and are now defined as hot spots in constant combat trying to suck each other into greedy right wing Black holes is truly flabbergasting.   It would seem the cosmos is constantly trying to redefine itself. And wouldn't you know it – but we are also players in this.

Is it by sheer chance
Or is it predetermined
That the entire universe
Is just timeless motion
Like all four year olds?

The only equivalencies we humans have here on earth with these rambunctious celestial combatants are our very own money changers, self serving politicians and unscrupulous insurance companies. They, like celestial hunters, have truly defined time for us all in a cage - and not a very big one at that.

As evolution ground relentlessly on and on, humans continued to muse and be amused trying to grab a sense of what time really is.

> And so it was, is,
> And may well forever be
> What does that leave?
> All that is in between
> The past, present and future?
> Remains illusive.

> History only tell us where we have been
> Be it tragic or comic
> Only the future
> Will tell if we learned anything
> From having been there.

Of course as time (if it exists) slithered onward and more sophisticated professional folks got into the game of "Where have we been?" And "What is next?"

> So - historically what is time?
> Since we don't know
> It is what happened long ago
> As for the future
> Opportunities abound
> But remember the clock may be ticking.

So there we have it, time and the infinite are undefined. They are like the basic geometric terms; point, line plane and space in geometry. You kinda think you kinda know, you kinda feel what they kinda are, but you really don't.

But now it is your Time to compose your own historical Viglets about time and infinity.

My Viglet on History & Time

My Viglet on Eternity

Finding Time

First thing to do
Is to decide what time is
But do we really want to know?
If we did then - what
Would we do anything differently?
Let us hope!

Trying to accommodate
What we know and what we wish for
Is about as inane
As trying to equate what we should do
With what we actually do.
So why waste your time?

For those who are dedicated "time nerds" the problem is further complicated by the fact that sometimes time seemingly skidders around. A typical Saturday example; your dream team is just two touchdowns behind, there remains only two minutes left to play, the stadium is out of Gatorade and toilets are all stopped up.   At this moment time stands still for everybody, players, refs, spectators and sponsors.

The internet and TV channels are catatonically reporting the news breaking event as though Armageddon has finally arrived as predicted by ancient ice gods with their frozen gonads and Foxy news. Newscasters (what a name) have their key underdressed ladies of the media screeching that time is standing still. Wow!

How each of us understands the concept of time, and we differ, the fact remains that it is most difficult to share, indeed perhaps impossible. It just may be the most defining characteristic of one's persona.

> *Sweetie: "When in hell are you going to clean the garage?*
> *Sweetor: "Soon as it freezes over Sweetie."*
> *Sweetie: "It just did."*
> *Sweetor: "Wow - global cooling"*

> *It is certainly true*
> *Our personal sense of time*
> *Is poorly related to everyone else's*
> *This is most discomforting*
> *Since now you and me*
> *Are always never on time.*

When having fun, time quickly slithers silently by without recognition. Kids can't wait for their next birthday. As aging relentlessly continues all the clocks speed up making us all believers in the relativity of time.

In childhood
Time moves either too fast or too slow
In middle age time requires "management"
In old age time is most precious
For all too soon it will be all gone.

So without knowing what time really is – you would think it is quite conceded to try and measure it. But that has never stopped our – less than humble species from trying. People have got to measure – everything.

Humans are indomitably
Arrogant, dumb and narcissistic
If they don't know something like - time
They for damn sure are going to
Measure it.

Early on animals, including humans, realized that when the sun came up it was time to rise, stretch, scratch, look for shade and prepare for happy hour later in the day. They decided to call this day and night. In other words, pre-happy hour (a prep period of lazing and relaxing) was called day and happy hour was called night. This was probably the original Garden of Eden concept that unfortunately went awry due to snakes and apples followed by sex and a later a hell of a shower.

We know that as early childhood science education classes for Neanderthals improved (no Neanderthal left behind) they all learned to watch the slowly moving shadow of a stick stuck in the ground as it inched around the stuck stick. This was really fun stuff - so they cleverly called it a sun dial and made all kinds of art work celebrating their concept of time.

Some day take a trip to Italy, or wherever the sun shines and look at all the sun dials. The concept is simple. Stick a stick in the ground so the sun can see it, and voile a shadow will appear telling you what time it is.

Sadly this stick in the mud is pretty much useless at night. Moon dials never caught on, primarily because the moon is cranky in sharing its light and everyone was either partying or sleeping at that time.

Later in history Rolex and buddies decided to add jewelry upping the sun dials costs appreciably – and they do work at night.

Now wouldn't you know it someone came up with the clever idea of letting fine white sand seep through a narrow tube? The inventor of this device then cleverly determined how much sand to use by comparing it with either boiling or frying eggs. When the sand was gone from the upper container into the lower, the eggs were done, depending of course on the kind of eggs. Dodo and Emu eggs require more sand than good ole bufforfingtons.

Not to be outdone another inventor with lots free time on his hands and felt dripping sand was beneath his social stature. Furthermore he had done well in his junior high shop classes. At first he decided to make clever gear, rope and weight arrangements but then moved on creating uptight springs that would make the gear cogs go clickety-clack. Each click would by golly be one second. Since the number sixty (sexsagesimal) was popular at the time, sixty of these clickety seconds became a minute.

Now that they had all these seconds they piled them together making bigger bunches of units. They created names like; minutes, hours, days, months, years, eons, till hell freezes over, etc. Today we can certainly appreciate the fun these early time keepers had in making up and naming collections of seconds. It takes kids years to sort out this lexicon, adults never really get it, so it remains a wash for all.

Enter the atomic age, splitting atoms to get a fantastic

mushroom cloud formation, and so now you can patiently sit and watch atoms take a dump and say that this is truly a piece of a nanosecond.   This radioactivity stuff tends to be quite consistent and so that has now replaced sand in a pipe - almost. Again keep in mind the nagging question does time really exist?

The latest time measurement gimmick is hauling all this time stuff equipment into space, at considerable costs to tax payers, to create yet a still better sun dial. It is predicted this sucker will keep time for billions of years. This will take the stress off the kids waiting for birthday presents - you simply tell the little nipper his present will eventually come from outer space.

However, great as all these expensive techno devices are, none of them really tell us what time is. They do keep scientists gainfully occupied while philosophers continue teasing them with questions none of them can answer. It is a hoot.

The better we measure time
A commodity we know nothing about
The more stressful times become
Because of times' uncertainty.

Zeno was a master
Of time paradoxes
He could keep everyone
Wondering who won
The hare or the tortoise
Or - was it a futile question.

These exciting hair raising activities at about time kept and still keep people's minds engaged and agile - and that is good - supposedly helps to ward off dementia and gout. Like Sudoku, word jumble and cross word problems they cleverly distract us from the fact that our bus ride is approaching its last stop.

To be distracted
May be very mentally healthy
Providing you have nowhere to go
But if you do - they are a total
Waste of time - which remains undefined
And that is of course why we love them.

Think of all the dreamy eyed people writing grant proposals to enhance and intensify this discussion about the nature of time - how brave they are. But if time doesn't exist they will have outsmarted us all.

Luckily, I guess, the media is still too self-centered, money driven and narcissistic to realize the advertizing potential on the meaning of time.

During a Super Bowl's half time
X-million souls move into a new dimension
Without the hoopla of a cold beer
Or dazzling fireworks
Truly wasted ad time.

Viglets to the rescue - express you intuits simply and without rancor or concern about the nature of time - is time your friend or your foe. We each have had many different encounters with this truculent concept and now it is your time to share with a personal Viglet.

Please share - thank you.

You know the drill - it is now your opportunity to create three personal Viglets on what you think time really is.

My Viglet on Creating Time

_____

_____

_____

_____

_____

My Viglet on Extending Time

Using Time

This chapter has a bad title, "Using Time", because you cannot use time. Time is an undefined gift, if it exists, given to each living thing, from humans on up to amebas and later of course eels, eagles, petunias, lichens and the gnarly Bristlecone.

Time is a precious gift
Given from an unknown source
It can be squandered
Or it can be cherished
We each must decide.

Every moment of every day we each make essential decisions on what to do next. "Tempest fugit" as elder folks in Italy would say.   And this was before airplanes were invented.

My oh my
"I am so very busy"
Said the harried greedy executive
Making money keeps
Me from finding time to pay my taxes
Truly mad and sad

Time is only found
By those who truly seek it
Dilatants are excluded
From this adventure
They are too damn busy.

The misguided notion that one can somehow find time is pretty ridiculous. Since we don't know what it is – or even if it exists – it would seem a waste to go looking for it.

But creative entrepreneurship marches steadily onward creating all kinds of "time" saving devices. These nitwits mean well as it was intended to enhance their "bottom line" and occasionally does improve the GNP, another really spurious idea.

Time is to be saved
As modern computer makers suggest
However, if time is non-existent
Then we haven't saved a whole lot
With these incredible "time saving" apps
We have sadly only learned to type
Generally with only two fingers.

So we eagerly succumb and recklessly purchase one of these clever devices to save lots of time for more fun things, like cleaning garages and toilets. The real "sucker up" of time is computers and their next their next of kin apps, mostly bastards in the traditional meaning of the word. You want to fritter away precious moments – get the latest app – it will find you wherever you are and require the rest of your simple limited life time to understand. The latest one is called "The Grave Digger". Not cheap, no guarantees but you can't be without it.

Harkin, said the Grave digger hawker
Today we have a sale on time
Totally without historical precedence
Stuff you don't need
Will never understand or use
But for damn sure today it is cheap
So get it now – while supplies last.

Let us analyze how all these time saving concepts work out in our modern, post cave, world. There are basically two scenarios.

Those who dream of a "Home Office" (as opposed to depot) complete with your own private water cooler filled with virgin Singapore gin and having an attached spigot for tonic. These are the neo toga wearers of the past, who now shun restricting underwear and love butt breezes.

Those with itchy feet and desirous of zooming around in hopped up rigs running on the fumes of innocent bovine later destined to become your medium rate fillet smothered in onions with fries on the side are certainly the most romantic, not to infer stupid.

Consider this conundrum
If there is time
How should it be used?
As a home office or
As a freeway vagabond?

Bottom line is clear, you first spend time earning the money to buy a mega monster with infinite app possibilities. It fits snuggly in your private parts. But first it probably has to be lovingly and tenderly unwrapped, plugged into adapters that require Chinese-English language skills. This task in itself is no simple time saving chore, but keeps in mind you are saving time. As one ponders this eloquent argument – happy hour thankfully looms – bringing sanity to all.

The moment of true ecstasy approaches as stringing wireless wiring, accompanied with non- insulating insulation and organic plastic doodad pipes appear to enhance (rehab) your dreamed for personal work area.

A quick flash back. There was a time long ago when this home office concept was conceived of as a barn full of cackling chickens and/or pooping cows that contentedly laid eggs and provided warm tasty cream enriched milk. Put the two together with ice cubes and you get true happiness as savored in ice cream.

Today this home office to be is now accompanied by noisy dusty jack hammers, honest sweaty day workers trying to become Republicans and discovering the damn thing unsafely fits the work area – and worse yet it doesn't work. So far the time you have saved is being challenged, eh?

Early in one morning after a drunken rambunctious night filled with abuse language about your time saving project you are ready and head out to the "Center of No Returns" with sales slips and guarantees printed in .05 Egyptian fonts tightly grasped in your sweaty palms. Your head is abuzz and throbbing but you know your "significant other" is going to whoop the bejeesus out of you if you don't go through this experience.

The return line begins outside in a cold wet drizzle. There is a blustery breeze that keeps the smoke from the jerk ahead of you blowing straight into your lungs. For sure this is uncomfortable, but another internal stressor gives you heartburn or worse yet – GERD. Once at the counter "Of No Returns" your request for amnesty is rejected because it took the rehab folks over 30 days and all your paper work is useless.

No question about it - you are stuck and sure as hell have not yet begun to save any time.

You now do what the gods have programmed you to do - cry, with lots of heaving sobs and copious tears. You have exhausted your supply of bad words. Last night's hooch has worn off and the raw edges of defeat are ripping you apart.

Then it dawns on you, that the worst is yet to come when your sig-other hears how you " made out" at the Center of No Returns. Your brain rushes to solutions, like, "Where ever in hell did I put those cyanide pills?

There are basically three "time obsessed" groups of humans. They clearly illustrate how diverse our out of the swamp creationism has taken us.

One group is just about all of us; it begins daily with the fact we can't wake up, then we drowsily fight traffic just to go to work, sit and do finger exercises all day just so we can later fight traffic to get home, fuss with family members, get upset with irrational Foxy news, struggle with restless sleep due to indigestible fat enriched foods and leaky personal plumbing, etc. For what you ask - so we can do the same routine all over again tomorrow? Yup. Pretty exciting, eh? These people have a clear understanding of the time concept.

> *It is off to work we go*
> *Not ho ho, but rather oh no*
> *Thrills come from QWERTY keyboards*
> *Longevity from rotten food and bad medicine*
> *And to top it all off we now got facebook*
> *To remind us all of each others plight.*

Whatever we learn the hard way
Paves our road to the future.
What we get the easy way
Is pretty much – useless.
This is a lesson to be cherished!
By all working stiffs.

The second time thinking group is much lazier, no gear heads here. They simply sit around in colorful terry robes all day, legs on chairs, tables or whatever, and think (so they say) about time. To them it doesn't much matter as long as someone pays the rent, like a working spouse, government grants and government bailouts.

The only people who know what these clever time thinking monkeys are really up to are the bankers (fees and interest), insurance companies (life expectancies) and an assorted bunch of unscrupulous ponsi scheme magicians (stock market gurus).

The third group of time manipulators, often rascals, is bought politicians, whose only definition of time is completely determined by their terms of office and adequacy of funds provided by sponsors. This group defies definition, so let it pass.

So there we have it. To some time is an undefined four letter word, except in cases like; it is time for happy hour. That we understand clearly, without hour glasses, watches or atomic explosions.

Your moment in time has arrived - how do you find time to do all the nutsy useless activities that eat up your life time allotment of time?

You are provided with two beautifully designed pages to express how you find time to do those things that are important to you. By the way this is the time that really means something to you. Bugger all on everyone else.

My Viglet for Using Time

My Viglet for Saving Time

_____

_____

_____

_____

_____

Legacty

We all know a few dimensions
Position, length, width, depth
There must be more
Let us hope.

The time sensitive word - posthumous - brings on a ton of emotions. Is that good or perhaps it is simply a recognition that we cannot let go of "presence", and need to define time differently.

What is gone
Is gone - or so they say
But maybe we are just to
Ignorant to realize
It is not gone, after all
It is just right behind us
So turn around.

Time and eternity
May be just about the same
They both portend a fantastic future
We cannot yet comprehend.

The words infinity and eternity are on occasion used interchangeably, but there is a difference. Infinity means going on forever, like a line is infinite in length. Eternity refers to the dimension of time exclusively. If something is eternal it lasts forever, like tooth aches, credit card balances and in-law idiosyncrasies.

Both terms reflect the indomitable human spirit that the game is never over, even if stout folks sing and your team is ahead.

There are times
When one hopes time will quickly end
But there are also times
When one hopes time will never end
May the latter be your dreams.

For sure
Life is often a chore
But there are also moments
When life is pure heaven
Like a soft purring kitten
In your lap.

Time will remain an enigma because humans are incapable of defining it – except for themselves. Trees and animals may or may not have this problem – they stoically and "gracefully accept" their time in the sun and with dignity move on, like being eaten by a hungry lion in the Serengeti at sunset or a bush dying from lack of water in Western Nebraska.

Time, Eternity and Infinity
Are undoubtedly
In complete agreement
Only humans do not yet get it.

The stream filled with moments we call time
Are about all we really will ever have
So why are we not better
At enjoying and protecting their eternal gifts?

The bubbly flow of time that we all float in will hopefully continue on indefinitely. But even with the limitations of human neural networks we must admit there exists hope for a future - joyful and eternal.

Since we have limited
Intellectual capacity
We must rely on our truly
Magnificent ability
Called – we believe.

If certainty does not exist
Then we by golly we need to admit
Happy hour may be as good as it gets.

Now it is your turn to express what becoming infinite means to you, your pets and your plants. This means you need to consider what life is and could that be the most important issue humans ought to address as our journey continues. Ok, if you are really weird you may create a Viglet for your favorite rocks.

I have a rock
It talks to ....
Dah - dah.....

My Legacy Viglet One

_____

_____

_____

_____

_____

My Legacy Viglet Two

Timeless

People say
Time is of the essence
I would suggest
Time is of the effervescent
It is always bubbling.

When it is gone
It is gone
So why lose it
When you still got it.

Who knows who we really are
No one – not even you
So why not start anew
By admitting we know little
And begin to savor what we have
At least that'd be honest.

Every component of whatever "time" is – is extremely individualistic. What we know today is minuscule and probably wrong. Perhaps we are all collections of components that may, or may not be deterministic, but we for sure had little input in making the "determinism" that made us.

Since we were helpless
In selecting our paternity
Perhaps we should be more humble
About having been selected at all
Think of those poor stiffs that weren't.

Time and infinity
May simply be two sides
Of the same coin
Flip the coin and see what comes up
In either case you are always a winner.

Giving birth to new ideas
Can be a bit of a chore
Since past experiences are often a drag
They must first be shed
So like a tulip bulb in spring
Newness can appear.

Old age remains forever a myth
To those who refuse to age
For them youth lies ahead
And oldness never comes.

A sure way to get jolted into reality is to softly tip toe through cemeteries. Personal looses resting quietly tear us apart. Then moments of the past become alive. History is relived. Names of those we don't recognize, now resting quietly next to each other, awaken awe as to what they were in their time. Time for us all has now vanished - so softly – we suddenly realize we are all still bonded by something called life. Time is gone; we are again together - eternally. Time has given way to the infinite.

Since finding certainty
Seems very uncertain
What remains is
Blind confidence
That there
Is intelligence
Somewhere
We just gotta keep looking.

Rest in peace – RIP
May indeed be a misnomer
Perhaps their new digs
Is anything but nappy time
But rather dynamic and timeless
Like the stars
Dancing around eternally
In unbounded time and space
Let us believe.

Soooooo---

When staring into that unfathomable
Abyss we call infinity
One has to ponder
Should I have been a Dem, Rep or Ind
Or does it really matter?
Oh, indeed it does!

The human mind is quite frail
Perhaps it thrives simply
Because it can believe
That in the end
It may be that only our beliefs
Really matter
And do become our eternity.

Let us not forget
Humans have three pounds of grey matter
The universe is considerably larger
And hopefully much smarter
So why not be a bit more humble
Enjoy and share whatever we have
After all ----- all we got is
Each other!

So fellow human vagabonds, drifters and nincompoops let us consider there may be a beginning or an end – we will never know until we get there – ha-ha.   Best be optimistic – look forward to a future that may be timeless, infinite and eternal depending on hope, faith and good luck.   But happy hour(s) is real - on that we can depend.

If time is timeless
And the infinite never ends
Then we need to hope for eternity
With lots of good stuff
Timeless and infinite.

Enjoy creating personal Viglets – that is your legacy. So – get on with it. Here are your guides.

Viglet for My Future

_____

_____

_____

_____

_____

My Timeless Viglet

_____

_____

_____

_____

_____

www.ingramcontent.com/pod-product-compliance
Lightning Source LLC
Chambersburg PA
CBHW020337290526
45785CB00005B/2065